I0753664

TWENTY POEMS AGAINST LOVE

AND A SONG FOR THE AIR

TWENTY POEMS AGAINST LOVE

AND A SONG FOR THE AIR

Poems and Photographs by

Chris Vannoy

and

Gabriela Anaya Valdepeña

DARKNESS VISIBLE BOOKS LA JOLLA 2007

First edition published in 2007 by

Darkness Visible Books
P.O. Box 577
La Jolla, CA 92038
darknessvisiblebooks@yahoo.com

All photographs, including the cover photograph, by Chris Vannoy. All poems written by Gabriela Anaya Valdepeña, with the exception of "Neruda," and "Road Traveled" written by Chris Vannoy.

The poem "Fictional Skin," with accompanying photograph, previously appeared in the online journal LanguageandCulture.net. The poem "Tanya" was included in the collection, *Welcome, Eavesdropper*, published by Darkness Visible Books/dPress in 2005.

The authors wish to thank Douglas James Martin for allowing the use of his couplet in the poem "Waiting."

Special thanks to Andrés Zapata, David Strumsky, Rudy Gonzales, Anna Zappoli Jenkins, Dan Adams, Linda Bower, and Jeremy Ray Vannoy.

FIRST EDITION

Printed in the United States of America

Library of Congress Control Number: 2007935997

ISBN: 978-0-9774000-1-0

Pero cae la hora de la venganza, y te amo.

—*Pablo Neruda*

CONTENTS

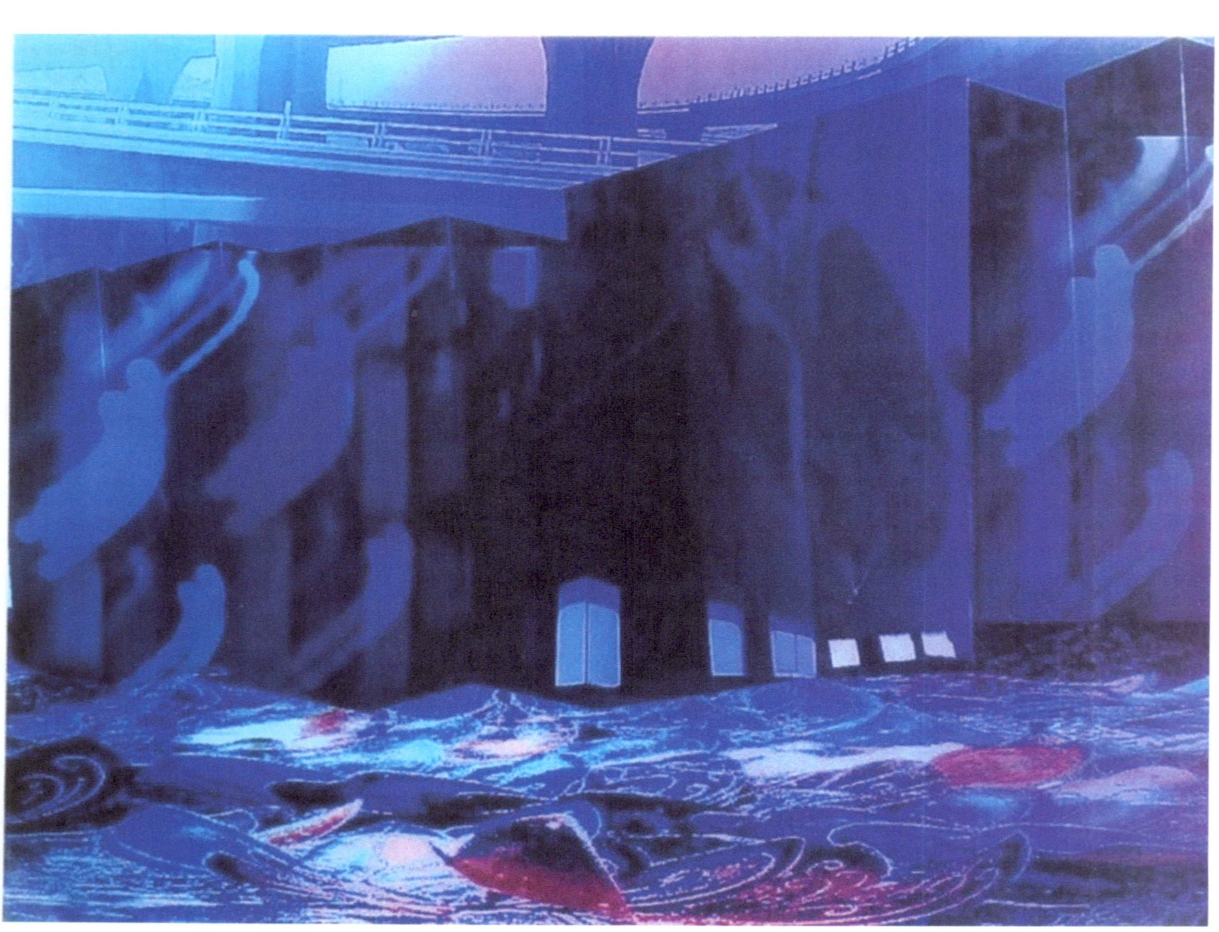

BLUE

Waves, with sharp painless cries,
lap at blind windows and mute panes.
All shades of blue bleed. I regret each kiss
I never gave to anyone who ever spilled
coffee on his morning paper, while I stained
your perfect face with my clumsy affections.
You loved me, as if I were a number
that could be multiplied and borrowed.
How will you balance time and boredom?
How can something that never touched my lips
leave such a bitter taste?
Crossing a slanted bridge from here to now,
we fell between the drowning edifices. The moon
hangs on our last words, turning blue.

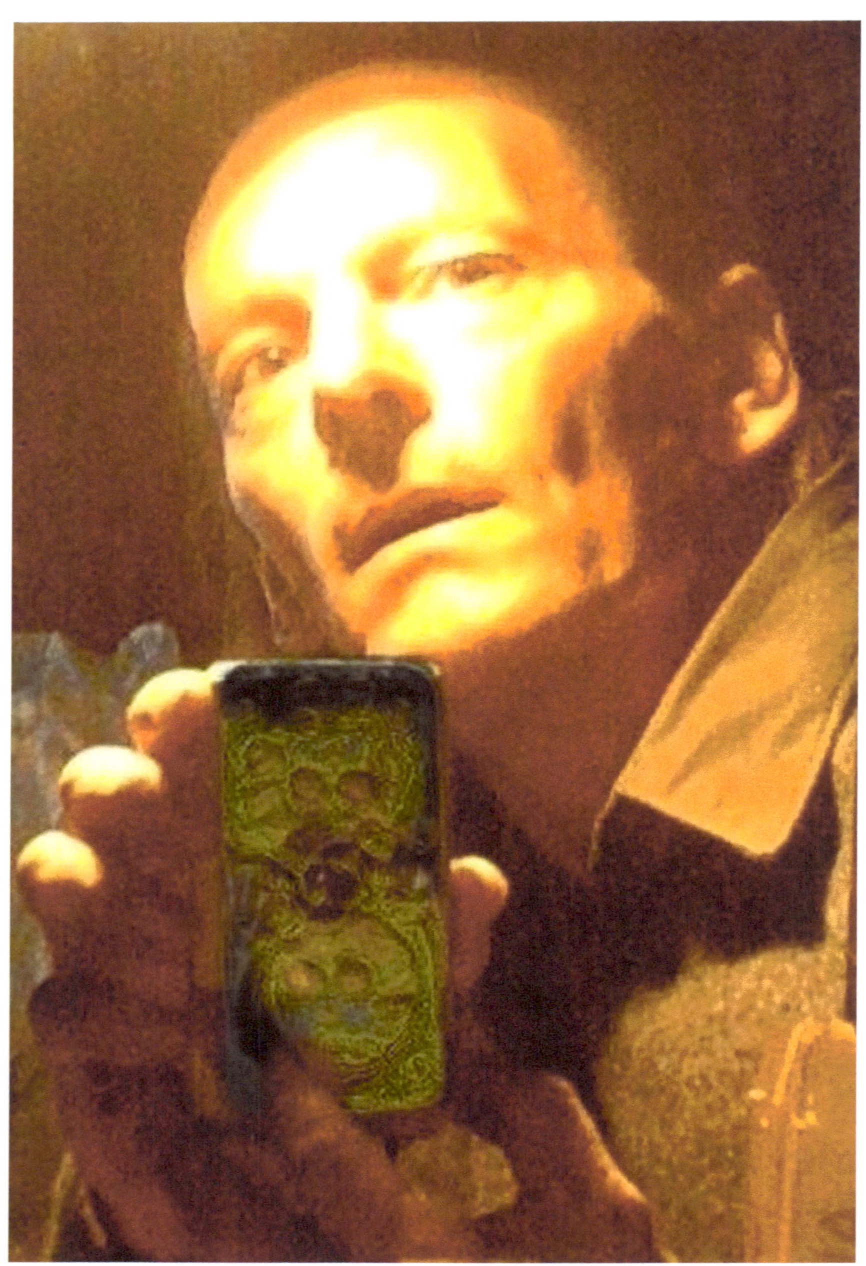

CAUGHT

Oh what laconic demon has unnerved me
with eyes certain as the grave?
What is this that tickles my sciatic nerve?

Sense and senses be obliged—
no sweeter deprivation have I known
than the thirst of your yellowed skin.

I have seen your soul
through your heart's lens traversed.
My life winks in your flash.

And I remember the lock of your hair
in an empty jar of peach jam.
I remember the whisper

of kisses, lies,
walks, and weathered bits of sun.
Am I a fool's gold digger

taken by a blind man
with an easy glare?
Offend me with verse—

in this dream of glass
your words are bullet-proof,
though I cannot prove your heart.

I shall look no further than
this *mise-en-scène*
leading to misery and mirth.

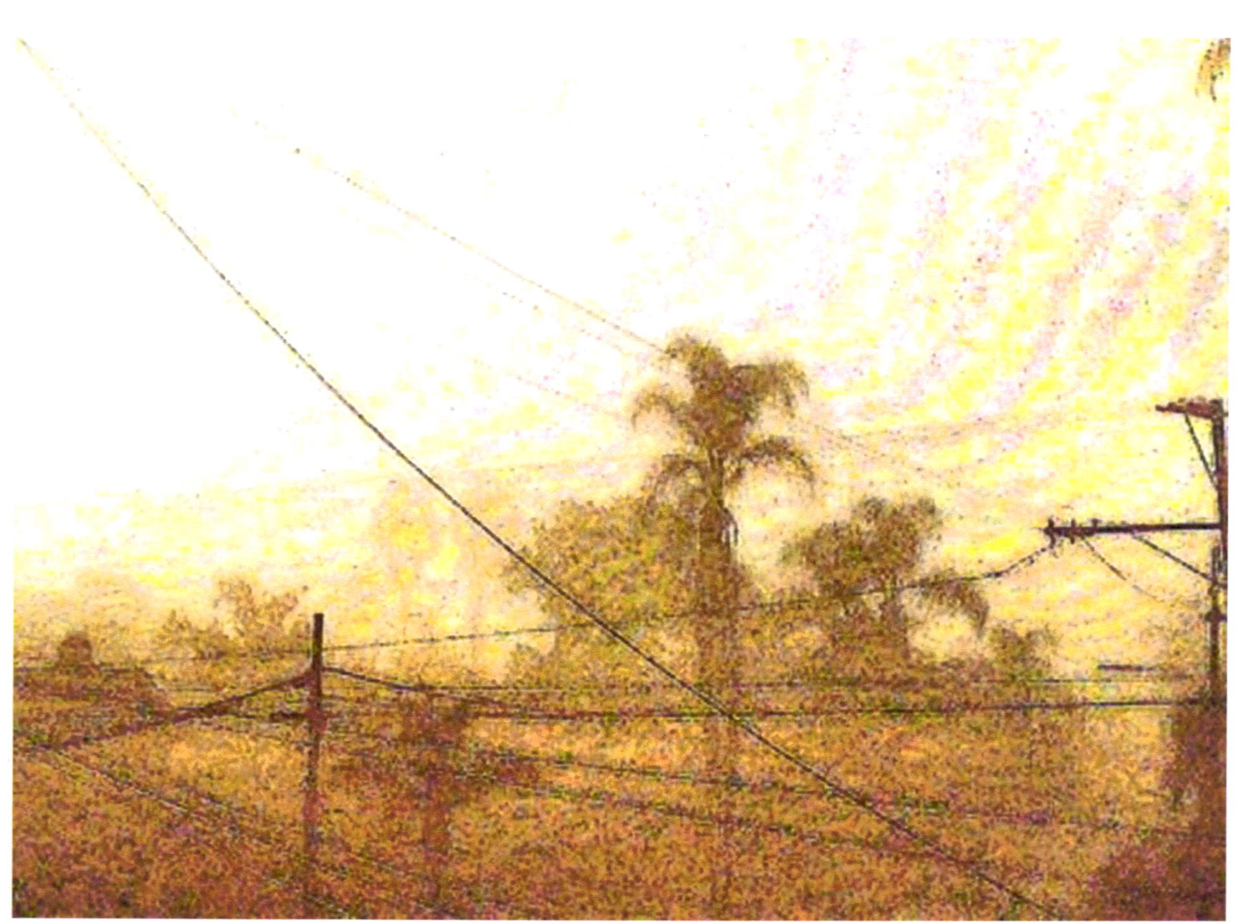

CINDERS

Heretic winds sing your *mea culpa* through my hair.
Your lavender and yellow cinders dress the sky.

My touch changed nothing!

You hanged yourself with my silk laces, which I had forgotten.
You died with my unheard words in your erudite eyes.

Now the young palms are mourning,
but the old ones know too well—

storms empty the lovers' reliquaries,
weaving their sighs through the gold dreams of May.

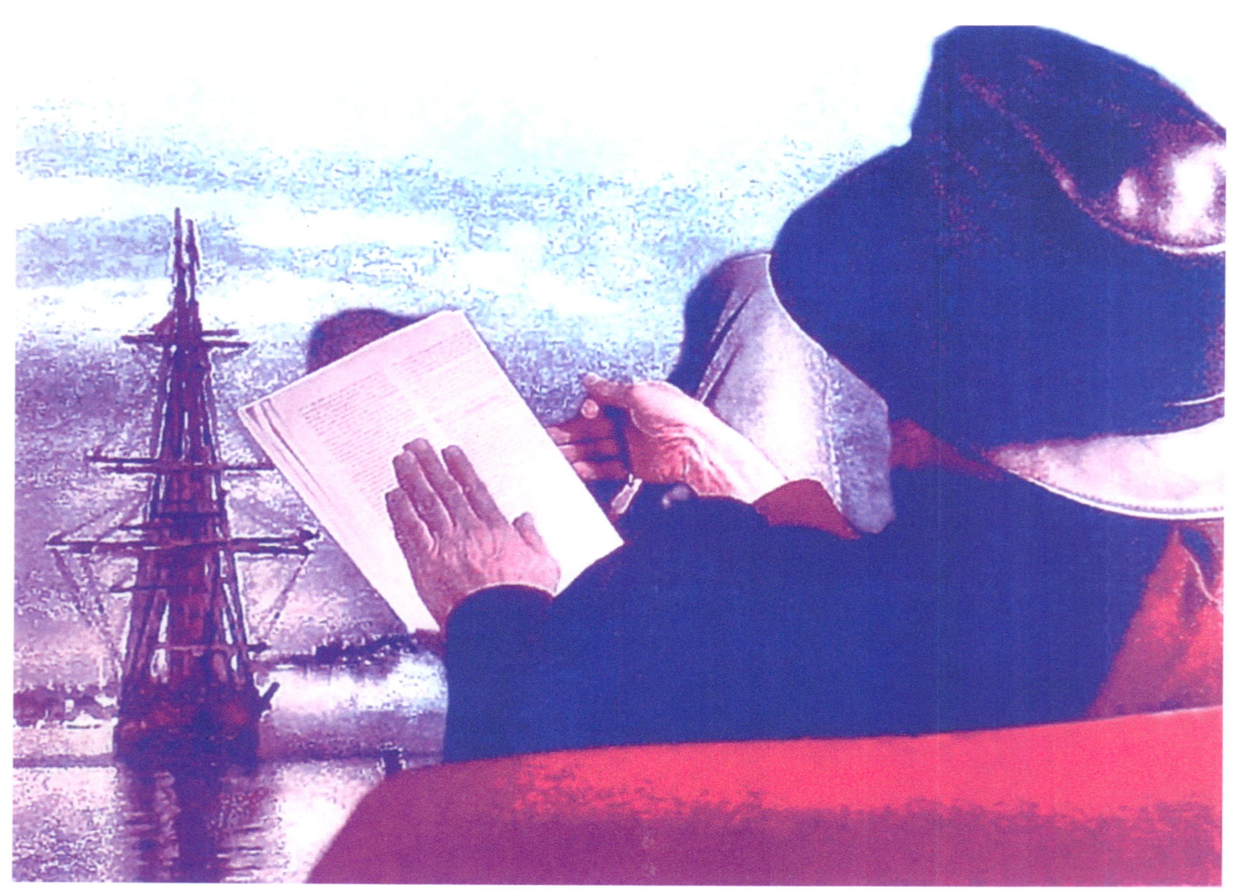

DAVID

Why are you reading me again? As the afternoon turns cold
my sails are anxious. I have cut the moon's chord.
I've discharged every passenger but you,
a peripatetic lord among pedestrians—
your old truck on the lawn collecting blossoms.
Your hat is your crown. Your hands sate me, and the sea
my only escape, has become hospitable.
I've nothing left to do but plant
a ring of fiery kisses 'round your neck.

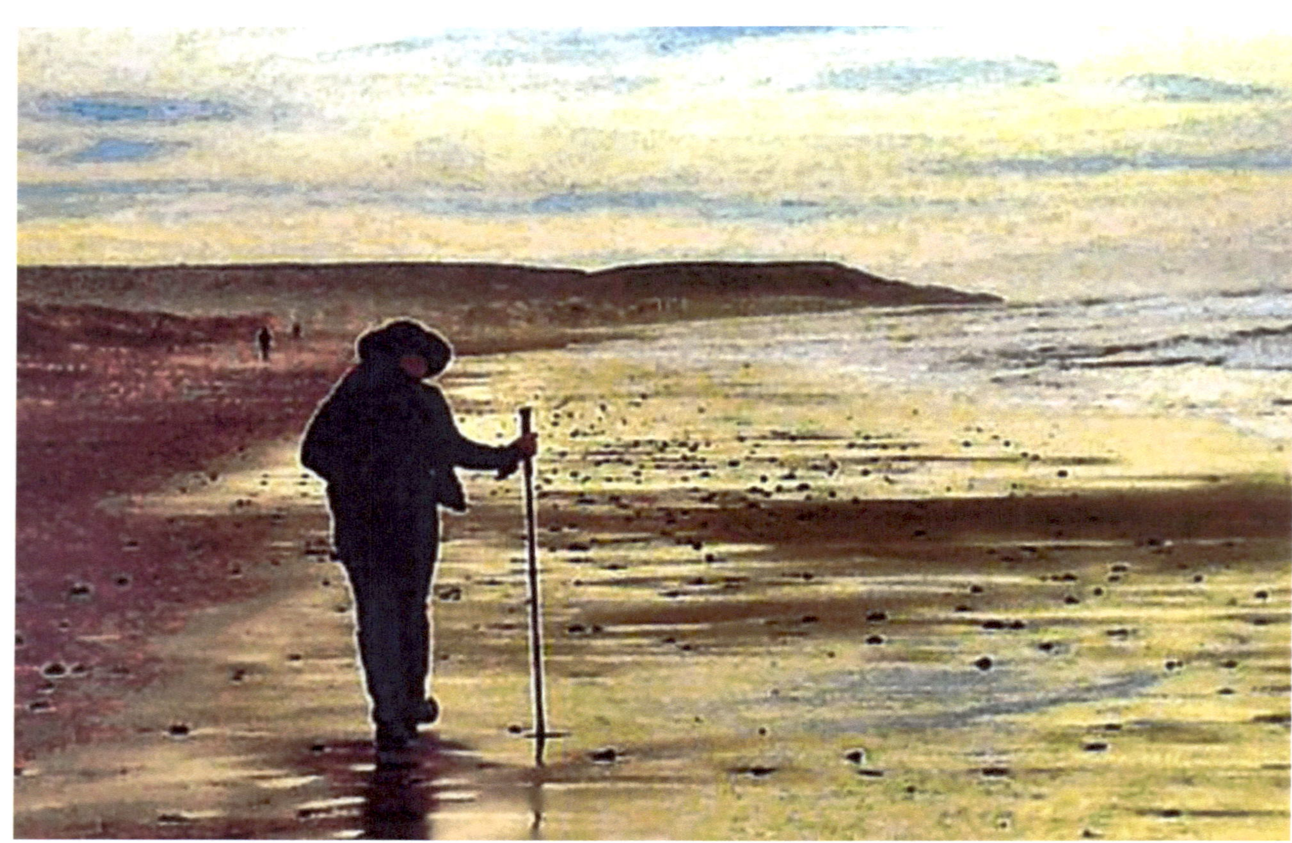

DISABUSE

I

How much I'd give to flatter you with remorse.

As my letter was in transit, I'd already begun
to forget how I dotted my i's with lamentation,
how my pen had limned a much brighter fall.

After a long stretch of sand,
you entered unannounced.
Raising your cane against me,
you let it fall at your feet.

Walk toward the white horizon
that has forgotten my name.
Curse the low tide.

II

Why didn't you hold me to my fury?
Why, when boredom struck,
did I exact my folly on a serious heart?

The stars blind my sad sleepless eyes.
What is life when all that's left are words?

III

You've come back, as only my words expected.
I slice the papaya, cutting my finger only slightly,
craving your mouth on my slanted peccadillo.

You've no longer the look of a lost believer,
but the eyes of a man who has taken back his heart.

IV

I take you as ghost, as man.

But I will not shower you with lover's talk.
Shall I wait until you've crossed the threshold?
I must not jump at the sound of the lock.

I will neither celebrate, nor renounce,
love's crooked path.

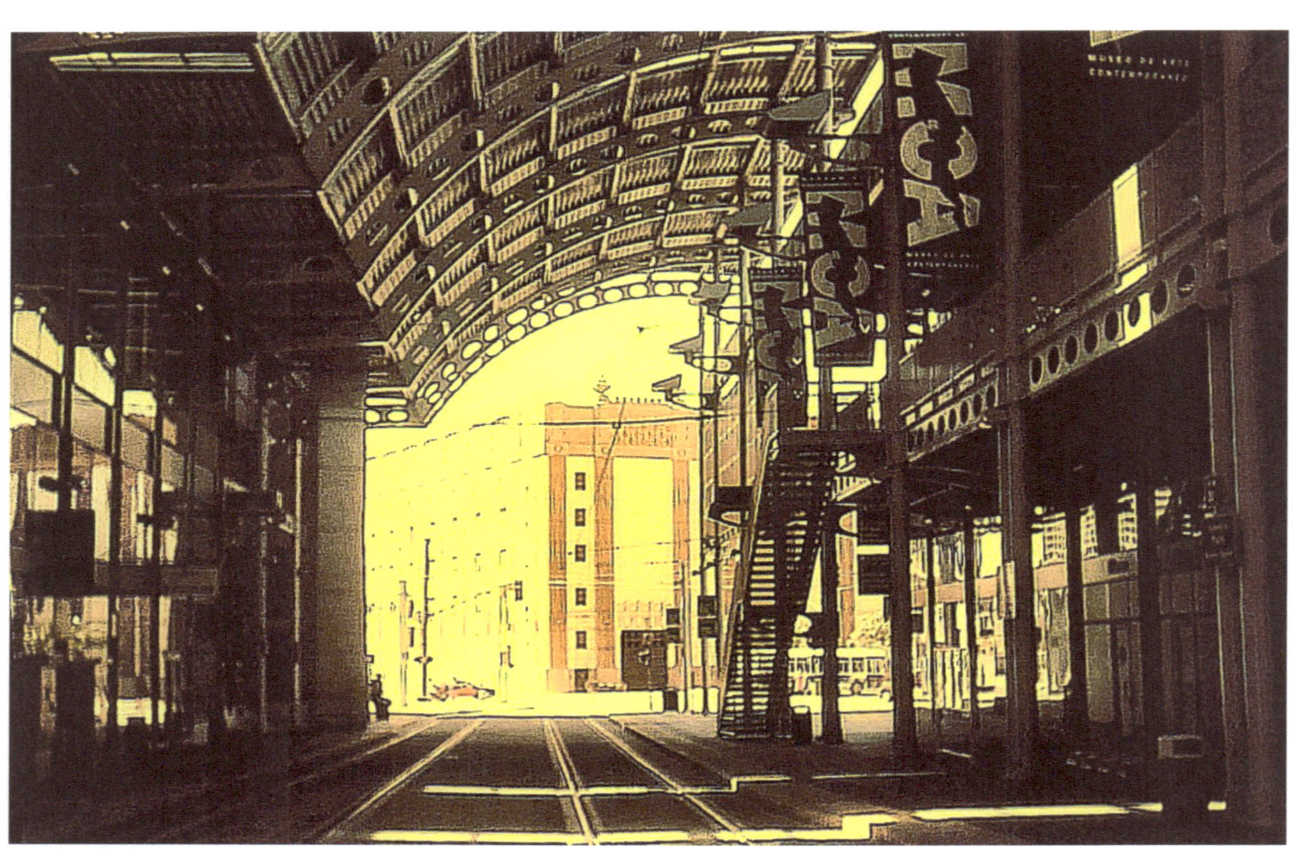

EMPTY WITH PEOPLE

Dare I look into the yellow face of afternoon, into the gaps
between your heart's stairs? The streets are empty with people
lost in desperate dinners. I remain abstemious. I dine,
while they shovel and split.

Happily, I put out the eyes of my rapist, and spit in the face
of he who faults my corset. May truth splay
skull and scrotum. Damn you

if you mock my dreams, for I fancy you love me
through rose toned glass. I meet you ash for ash. I wake
in the third act beneath the theater sign, while you press
your hands in concrete. At night I hear

ghosts trade life stories from their sleeping bags,
counting the ignorant stars. I am looking-glass and quicksilver,
hourglass and sand. From this dry street, the sea

remains my deliverance, should Alice ever stop
asking for breath.

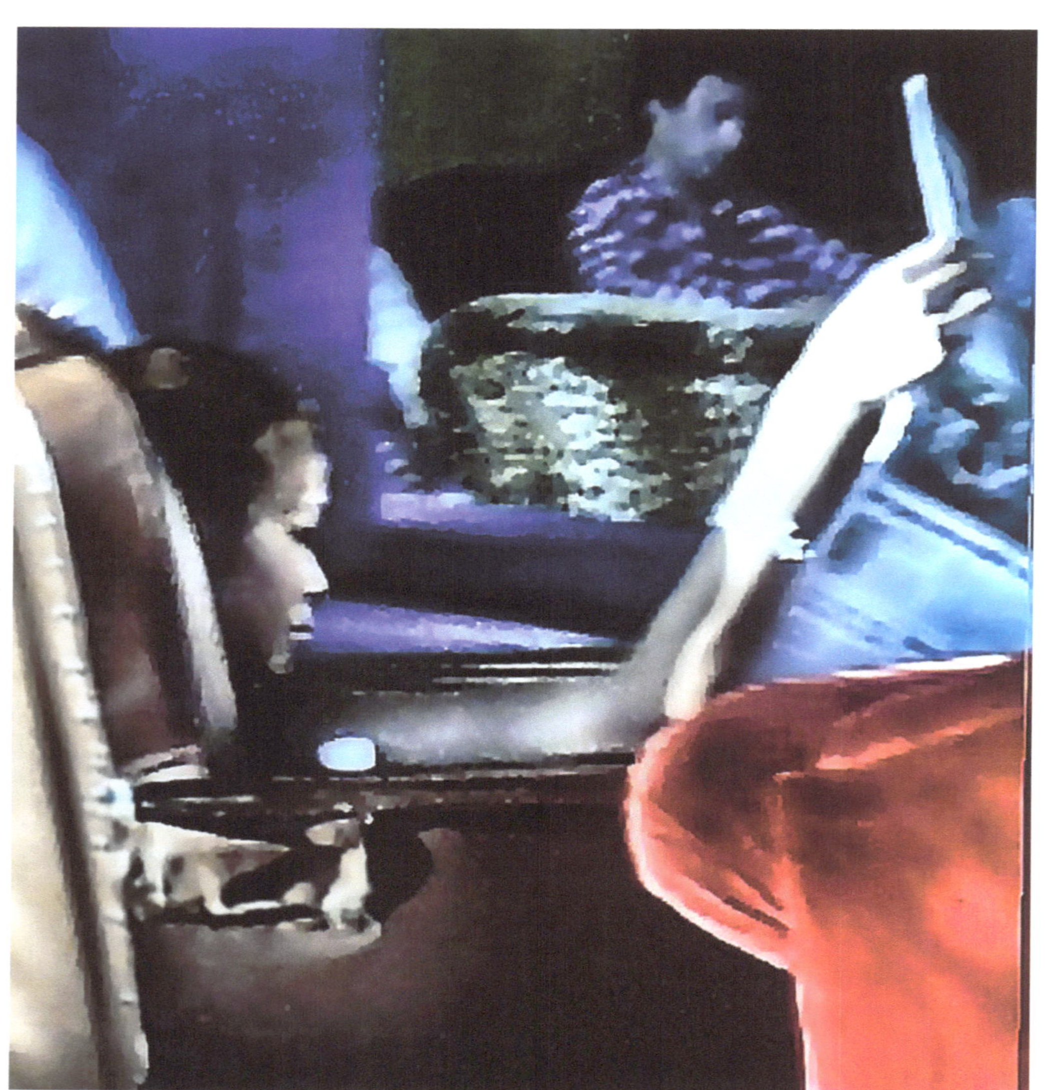

FICTIONAL SKIN

I was made to stumble over your sentences, to seek
the freedom of your cage. How could I not be the one
to draw out the blue in you, to resurrect your nobility,
to barter with the wind for your hearts, entombed
like Petrouchka dolls? I will dress you in newspapers,
so I will not be tempted to read you. I am in love
with your pupils pitted against the dark, with your fictional skin
framed by the moon's laughter. Wiles would win
your love, but I am too disturbed by the orchid missing
from your hair. I will not quail. I call my breath to arms!
I will ford your apathy with a kiss to four blithe fingers,
though I plant, in your quintessential thumb,
the seeds of suicide.

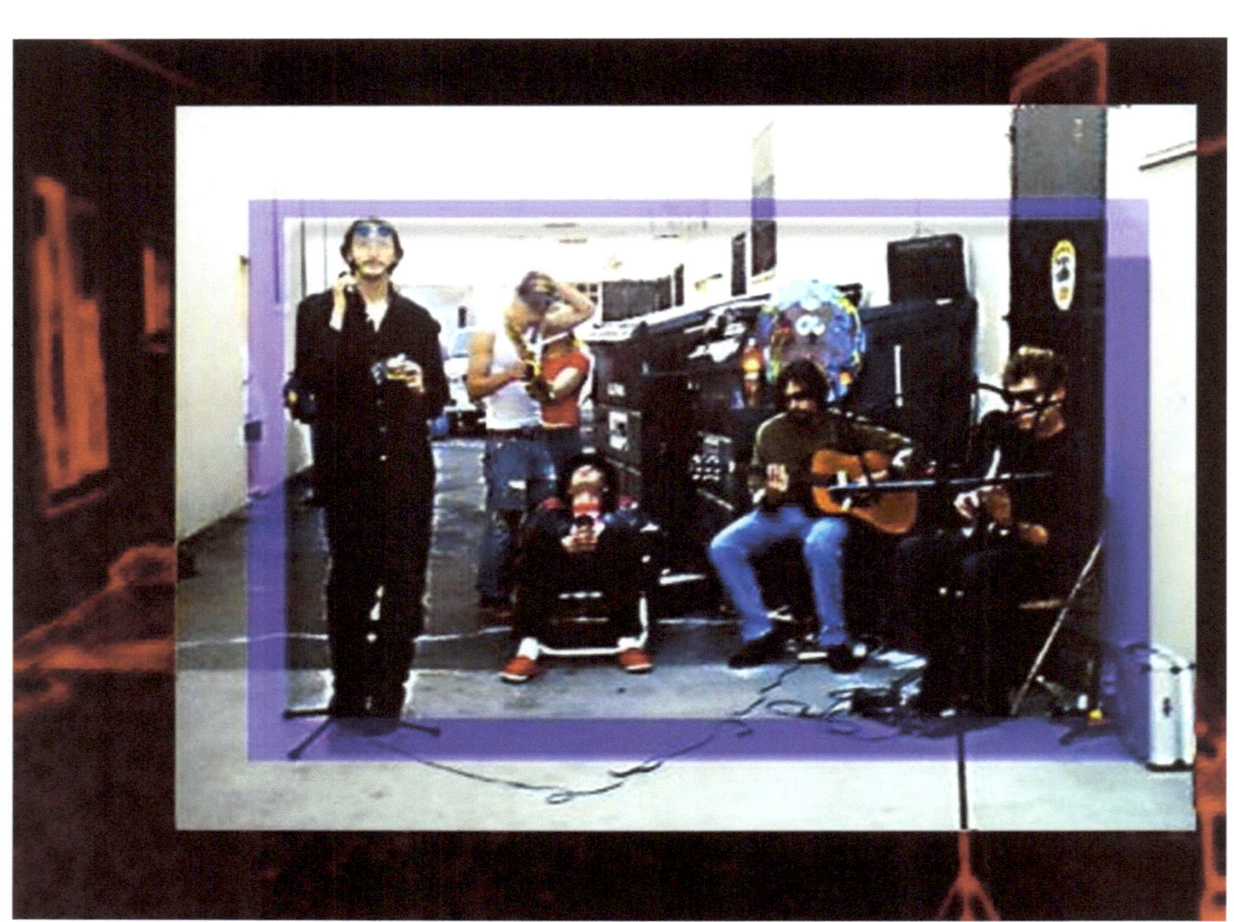

HEY RUDE!

Tall drink of heart-ache!
Don't you remember—
I squeezed oranges for your vodka?
I taught you the first steps for your salsa?

Drunk we danced while empty planes
soared over the party, while the record skipped
and the deck shook and I was sure
I took your breath.

Hey Rude,
if your heart were plastic and your dreams
dough, I'd still give all
for your trifling kiss.

You're highballin'; you're singin'; and I'm
not crawlin', just askin'
when you would have given
your borrowed drum to know
I was not married to that Greek.

You offered me your coat
seconds too late,

my wealthy shoulders denied your bare
threads of bohemian vanity.

Ah Rude, it's just as well.
You took my charity and bought
cigarettes to last 'til Monday.

You're too tall, after all, and I should not want
your number, your digits, your mathematics,
or your mouth.

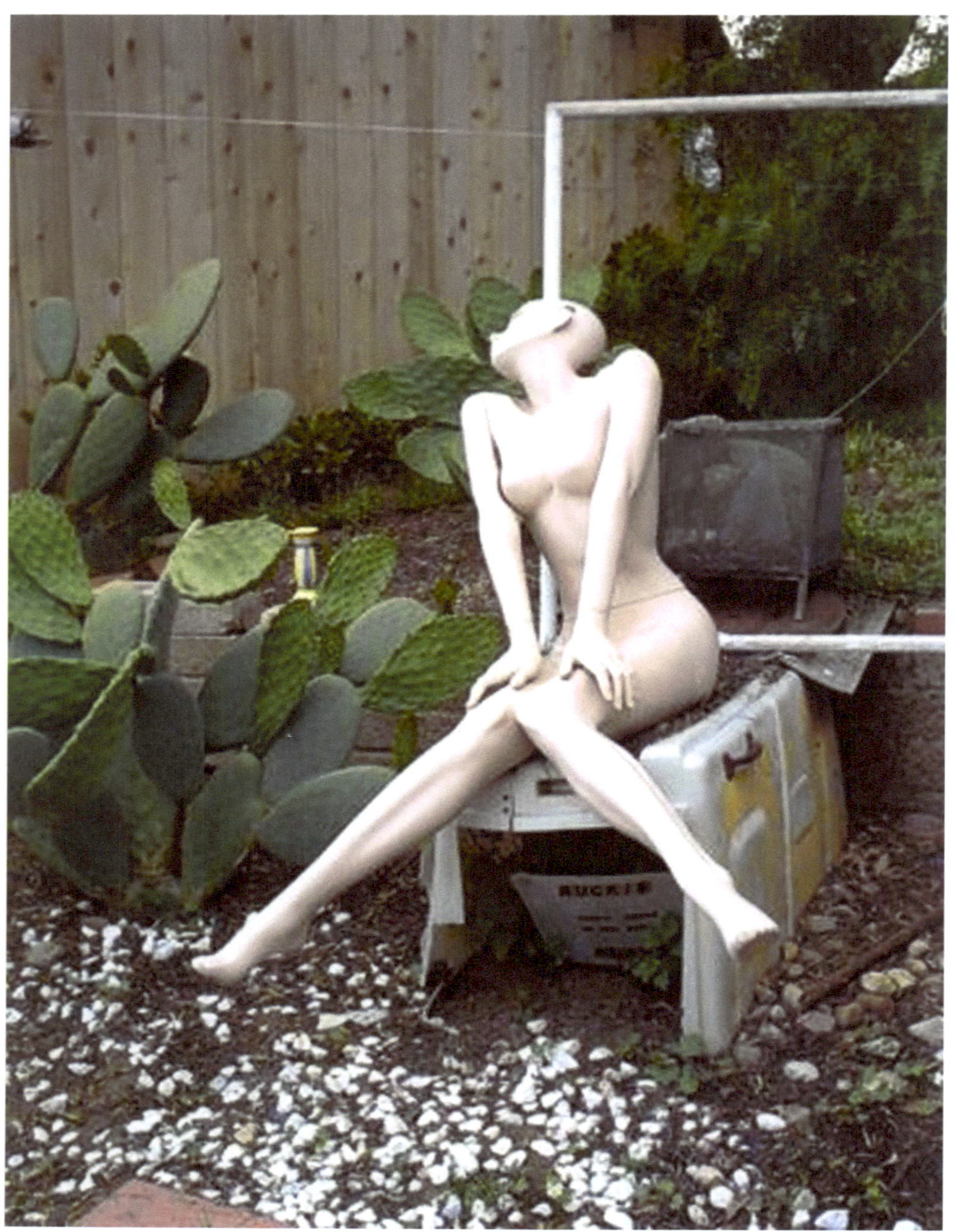

HONI SOIT QUI MAL Y PENSE

No moles have I, no hair, no lash, no brow, no
shame. Drunk on cactus juice, drunk on infamy. Ha ha!

I sing the blues naked in the sun. I sing the blues naked in the sun.
But when it rains, I'm quiet as truth, shy as a pickle
in the bottom of the jar. Oh, I am only playing

my part—which you wrote, after all, though cursorily,
half aware. And now the scene makes sense, breaking you
like that grey whale's song. Hide away and bleed. My heart

stopped long ago, and that is why I'm laughing.

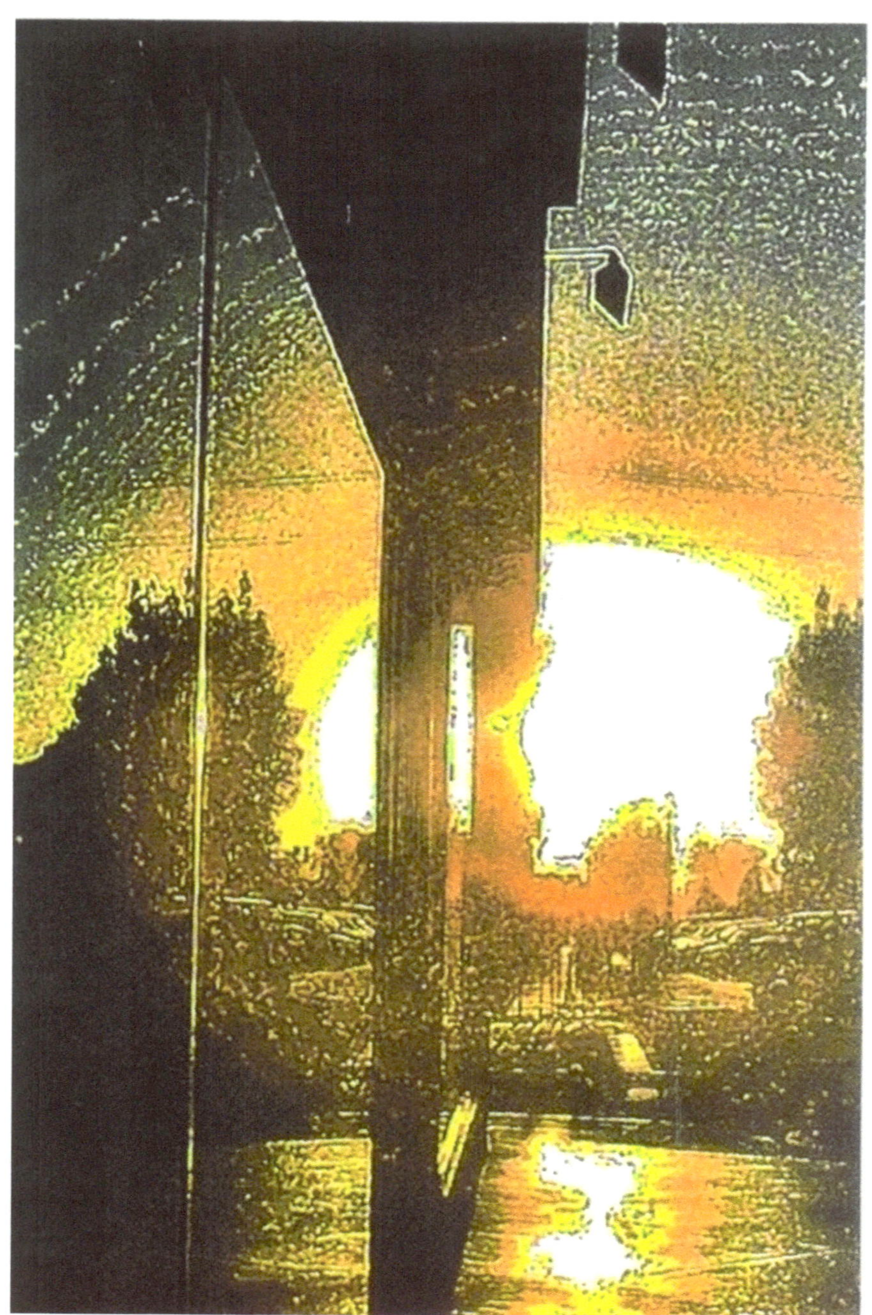

I COULD CRY

Sunday I rode out without my hat, with the weight
of your broken violin on my heart. But I tread on,
as the doomed often do. I vow to smoke

one cigarette in memory of ashes, and cloud
my plans with smoke and streetlights. The box cars
are full, and everyone sings . . . *I could cry*.

These power lines lead to Hell's anteroom. The sun's
edge bleeds time, while rain blurs yet another covenant.
Every miracle spends the magician. Tap

your wing-tipped shoes on the stairs.
I've come back, ready to cash in
my birthday wishes, for one kiss and a lie.

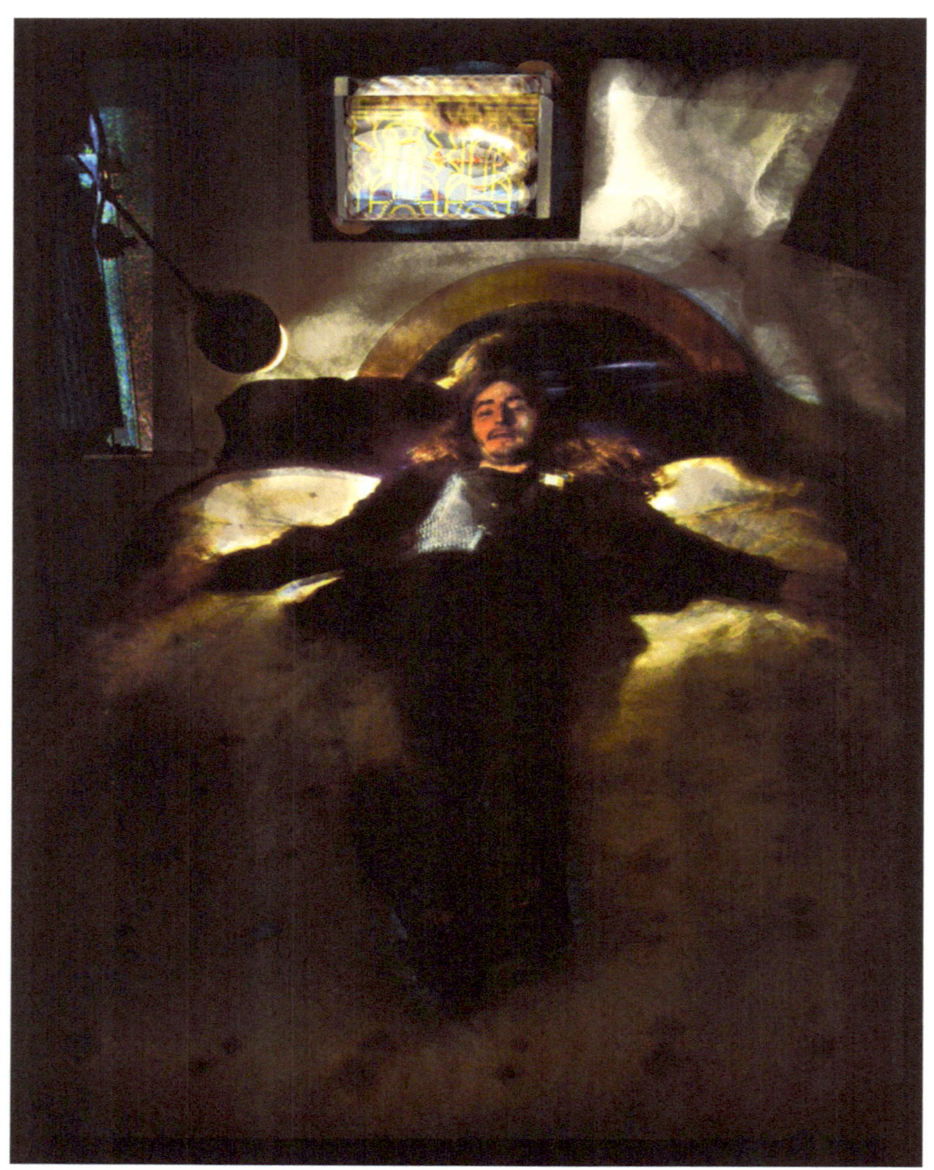

INDOLENT CHRIST

You've angels to scold, and another suicide's note to edit;
yet you lie, supine, on my Sealy Posturepedic,
smarmy, smug, smelling of rose water,
listening to the Book of Life on tape.
But what of those names yet to be written?
I've puffed your pillows ad nauseam, snapped your enraptured
face in the morning's shadow, your arms spread wide
like a lazy river of flesh. I've hung and rehung
the pietas as you asked, high then low, and fed you
rhubarb pie, wiping the spilt milk from your chin.
I should spit your lukewarm kisses from my mouth!
I don't want to know how to love you anymore. I'll leave you,
I swear, for that restless and charming Satan!
And what shall I say to the indolent shepherd's flock:
Let them read Blake?

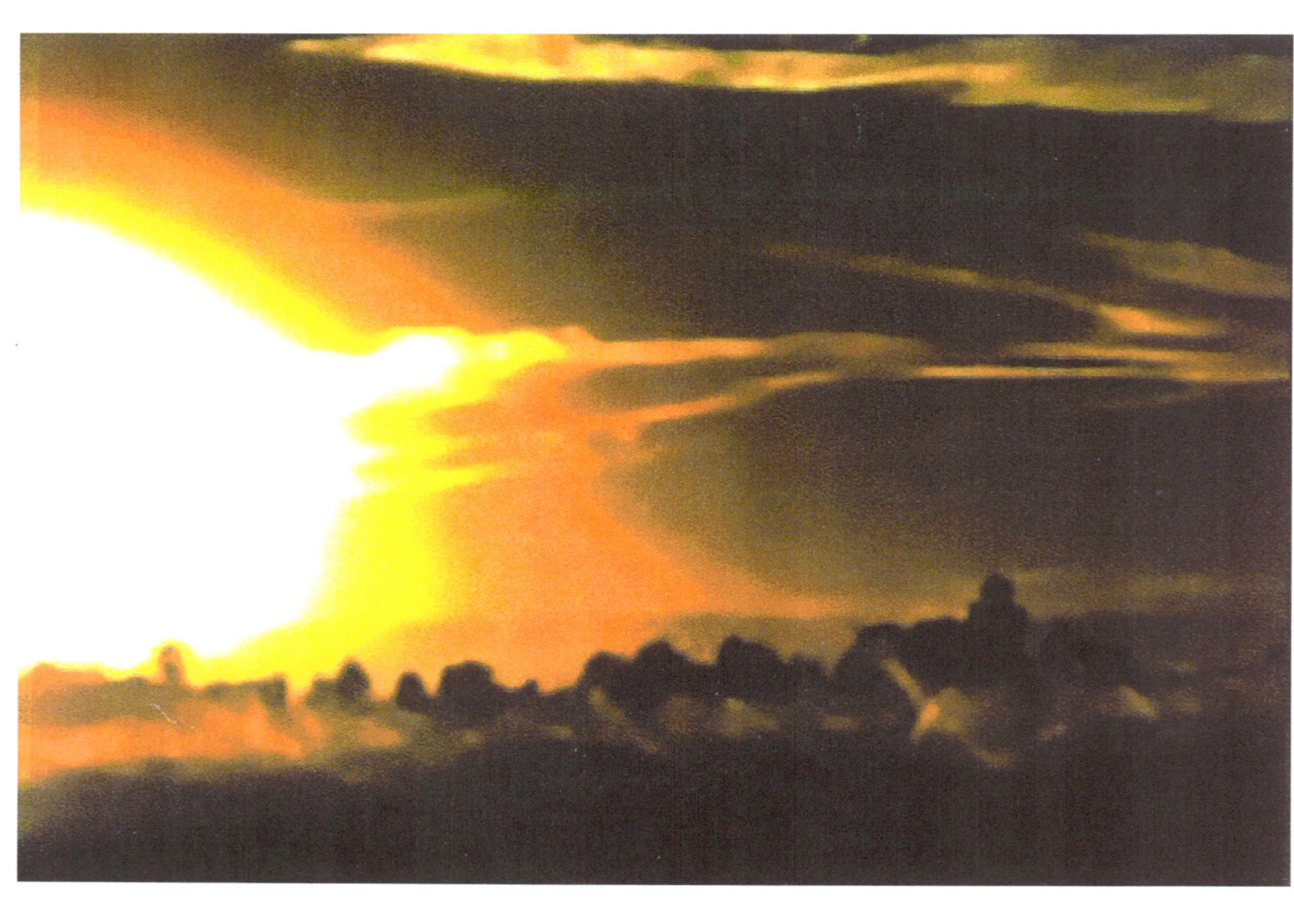

LASHES TO THE SUN

Only that deep god within knows how you tame these wild tears.
Bind me with the cello's strings as I have wrapped you in my veil,
gagging you with syllogisms, while lazy gods slept in moss.

The orgasms you ration mount for me in heaven. Still, I tremble,
here in your arms. Our quilt is made of words. My gypsy skirt woven
in your fingernail's half-moon, while I tie your lashes to the sun.

Ride away with your backpack full of poems and appointments.
The women you have made of me
will keep you faithful, yet alive.

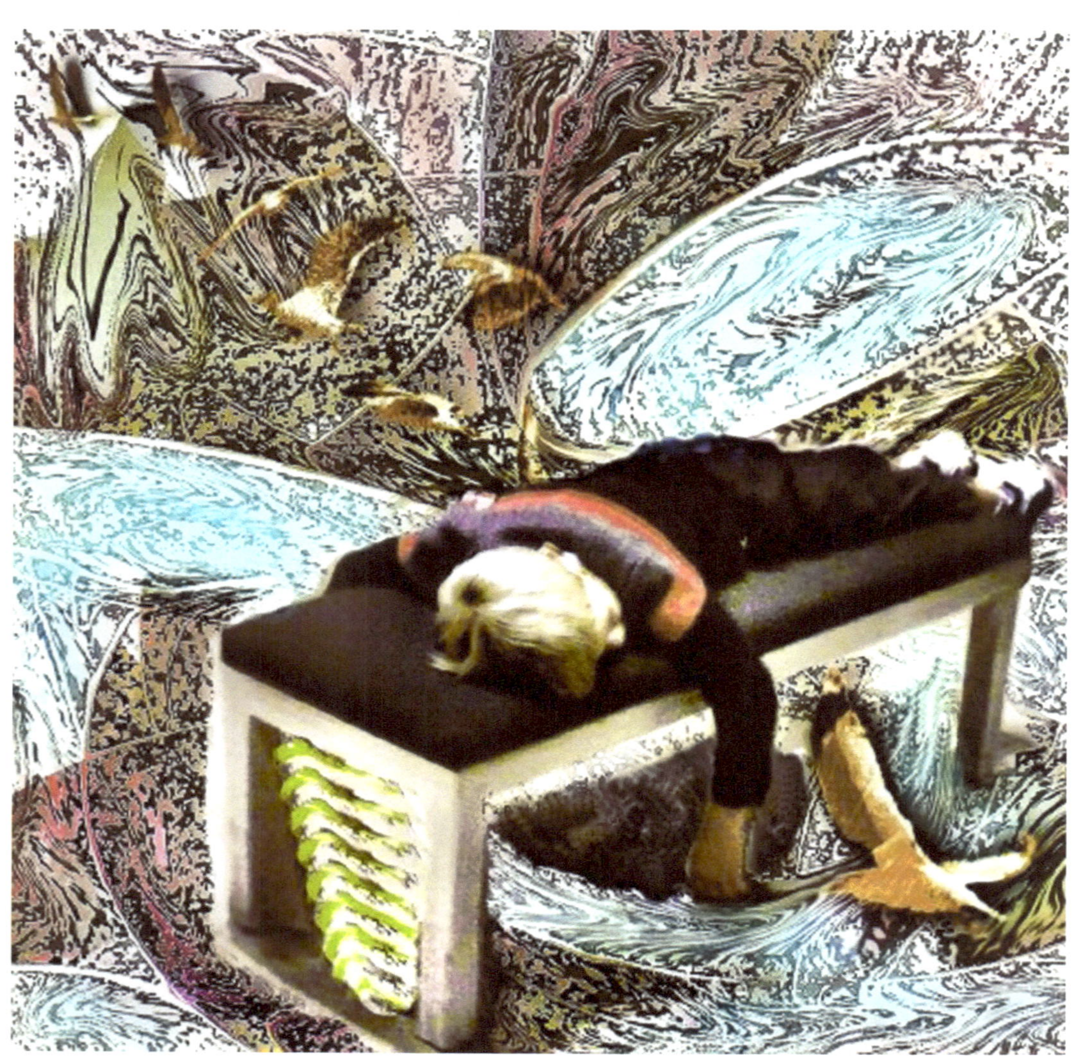

NERUDA

Fires of birds
swim from the dust of his feet
and he tells me
the journey's just begun

His socks lie warm
near my bed
next to locomotives of steaming villages
in a pot of stones and blue sky

A stream of feathers and clocks
ask me where he has gone
I tell them
he is sleeping in libraries
between oranges and melons

I tell them
tomorrow he will walk
in countrysides of mirrors and dreams

When they find him
their mouths will be filled with canaries
a dance of bones
will whistle
when he is near

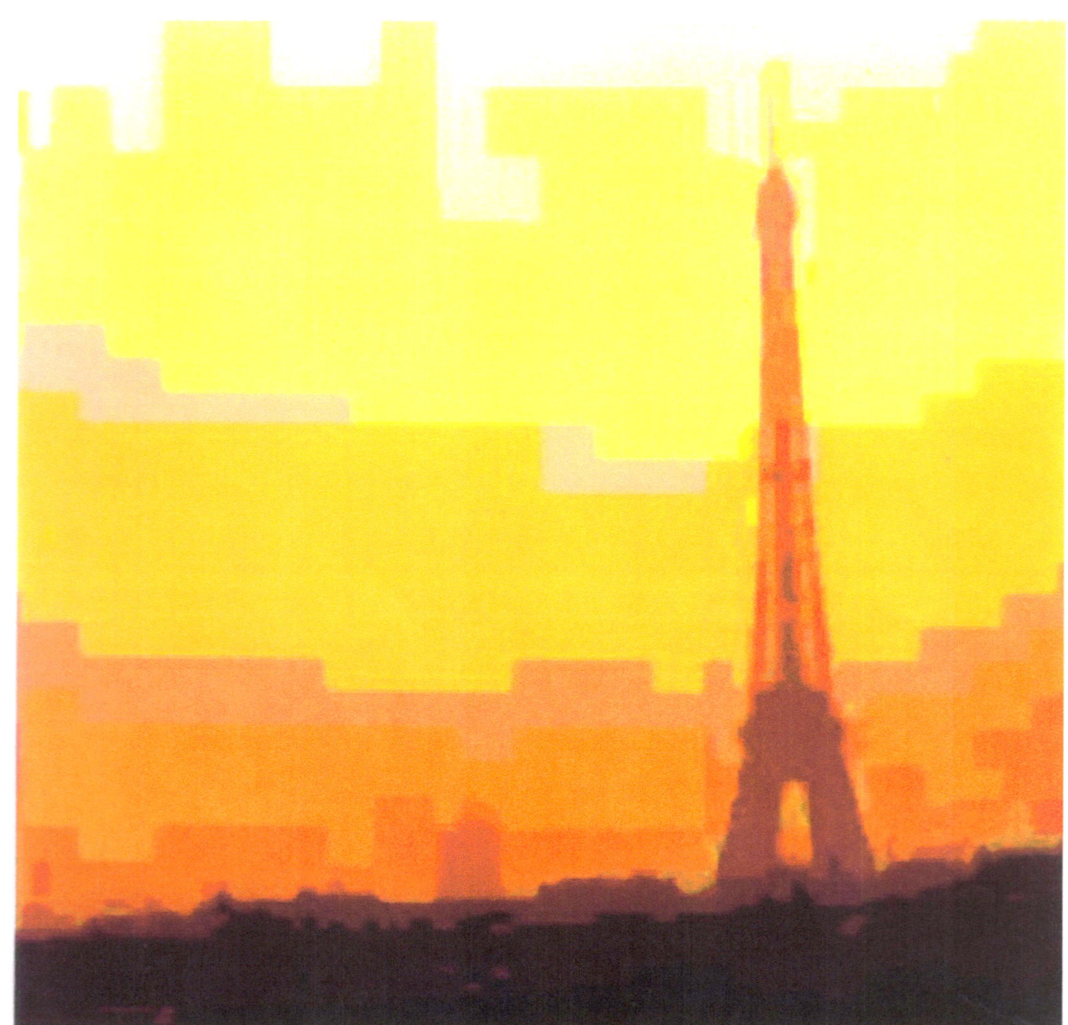

ROAD TRAVELED

She is sad now
reaches her hand towards mine
and tells me
there is a restlessness in her
talks of Europe & New York & New Orleans
& of leaving this place that saddens her
where the days of the year grow longer
rush swiftly by her
call for the movement of her feet
to catch the moment in her heart
where she looks back at me
to wonder where I will go
when she is gone

I watch as she paces
the cage she has built around herself
and gaze at the green grass she paints
through the broken picket fence
with a long brush on the end of a wooden stick
and I ask her if she knows that the paint
will crinkle and fade when she is gone
and I am here

I crumble printed pages into a ball
toss them
one by one

into the wire mesh metal basket
one by one
they find their place
where gravity and consequence
stop their bouncing roll

And I think about taking
a picture of this pile
to give to her for her trip
and of telling her
that I will be here
waiting

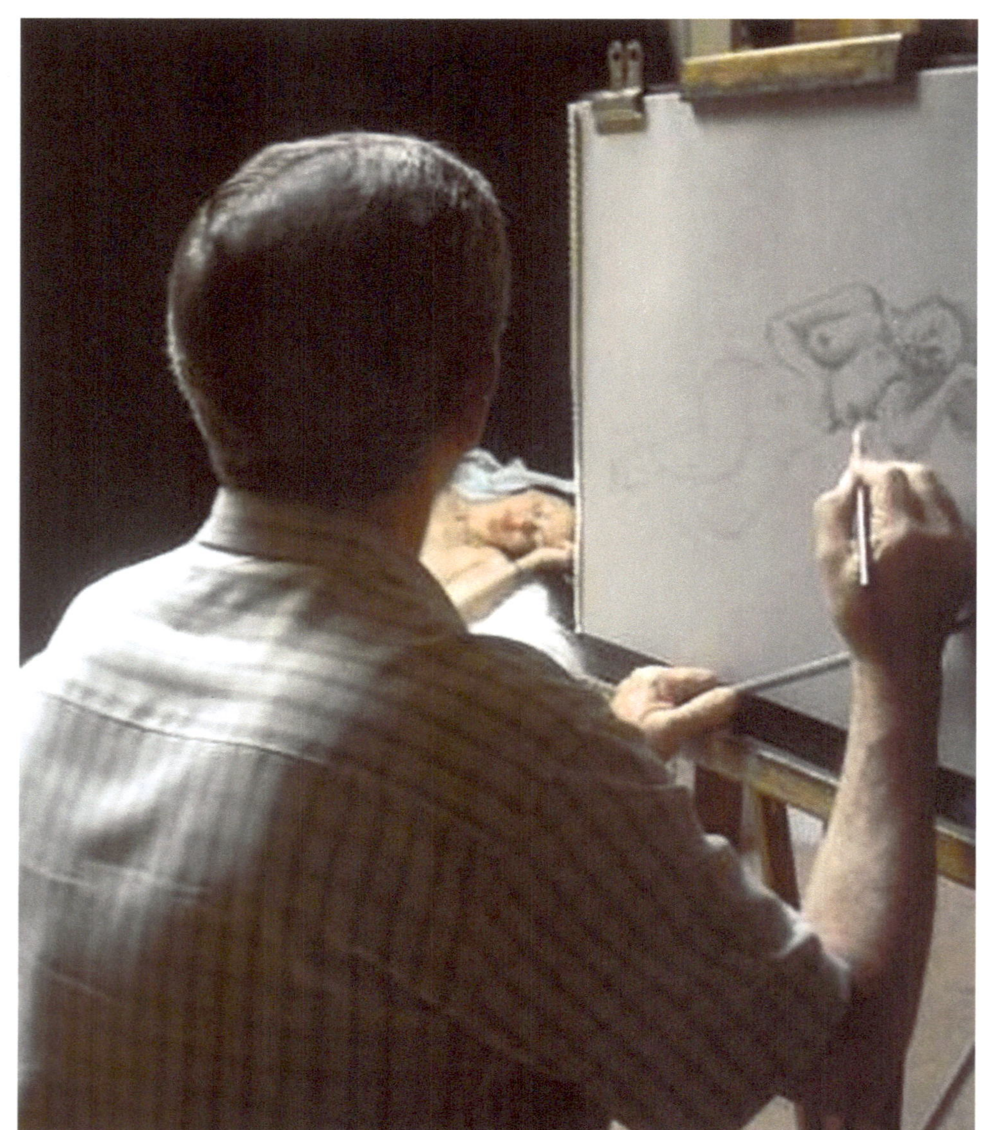

SLEEP ME AWAY

Busboy! Bring me some water, bring on the hurt!
I will cast you out like an old whore, or yesterday's software.
I build ladders to God from paperback westerns, and men like you.
What good is wine, if you won't drink? What good
the hearth beneath your stone feet?

Shall I bless the impertinent sea bird that keeps you
from sleeping me away? Oh, the pills you vomit! I spit
on your piano; does it still lean craftily to the left?
She, I—I for an eye, heart for a wafer, soul
for the chasm between your ribs. Yes,
I miss the train's whistle and the track's song,
burrowing in your bed while you pretended genius. I miss
your love letters, though they line the cage of the parrot who mocks you.
Have I scared you silent? Shall I send greetings to your mother
from my dead father? Shall I salute the amber-haired nymphs,
who must now endure the same dances, the same vertigo,
the same chatter of lesser angels?

You will inherit only my empty veins. My blood
belongs to the mosquitoes who cannot help themselves.
I am lost as a radio in the desert, broadcasting drunkenly to the sand.
I know you would make melody of this, singing my words against me;
then I should be deaf. I know your eyes would be the sea's religion;
then I should be blind. I will not hear, nor see, nor tidy my closet.
I shall set the past on fire.

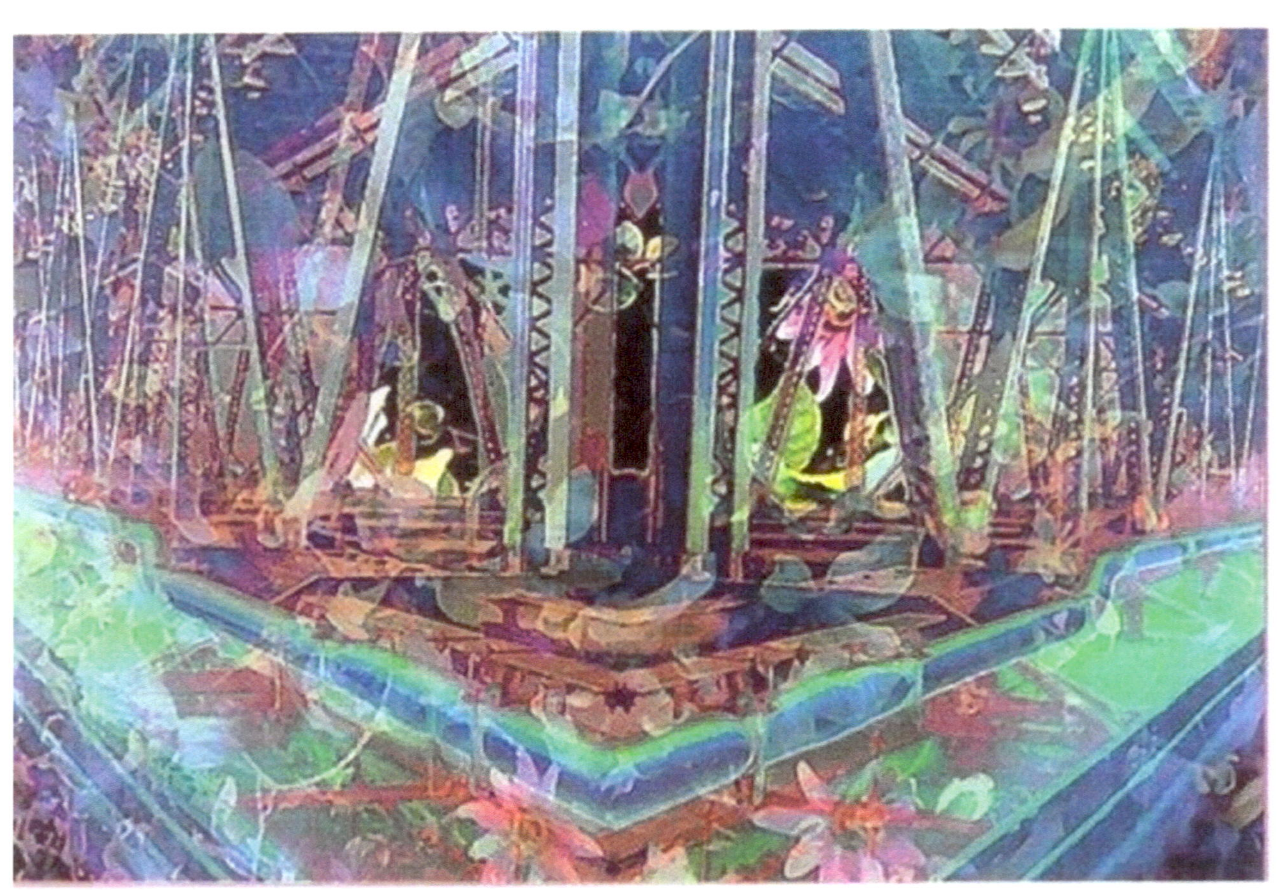

STRANGE FEET

Hear the caterwaul of your cat, the taunts
of azaleas you never gave. The night
sweats sugar blossoms. Meeting is sorrow, now
that the dream has been redeemed. How long that ticket
lingered in your trousers, washed and dried
a thousand times, while the numbers remained almost
readable! Oh my love, my mirror image,
how can I bare myself before you here
on this psychedelic stage where peccadillos
grow strange feet and a stallion barks. The light
attacks us now and we are wounded beyond
our comprehension; though allegory assuages,
and once again we are whole to strike the sun,
which falls and breaks in a million fiery hearts!

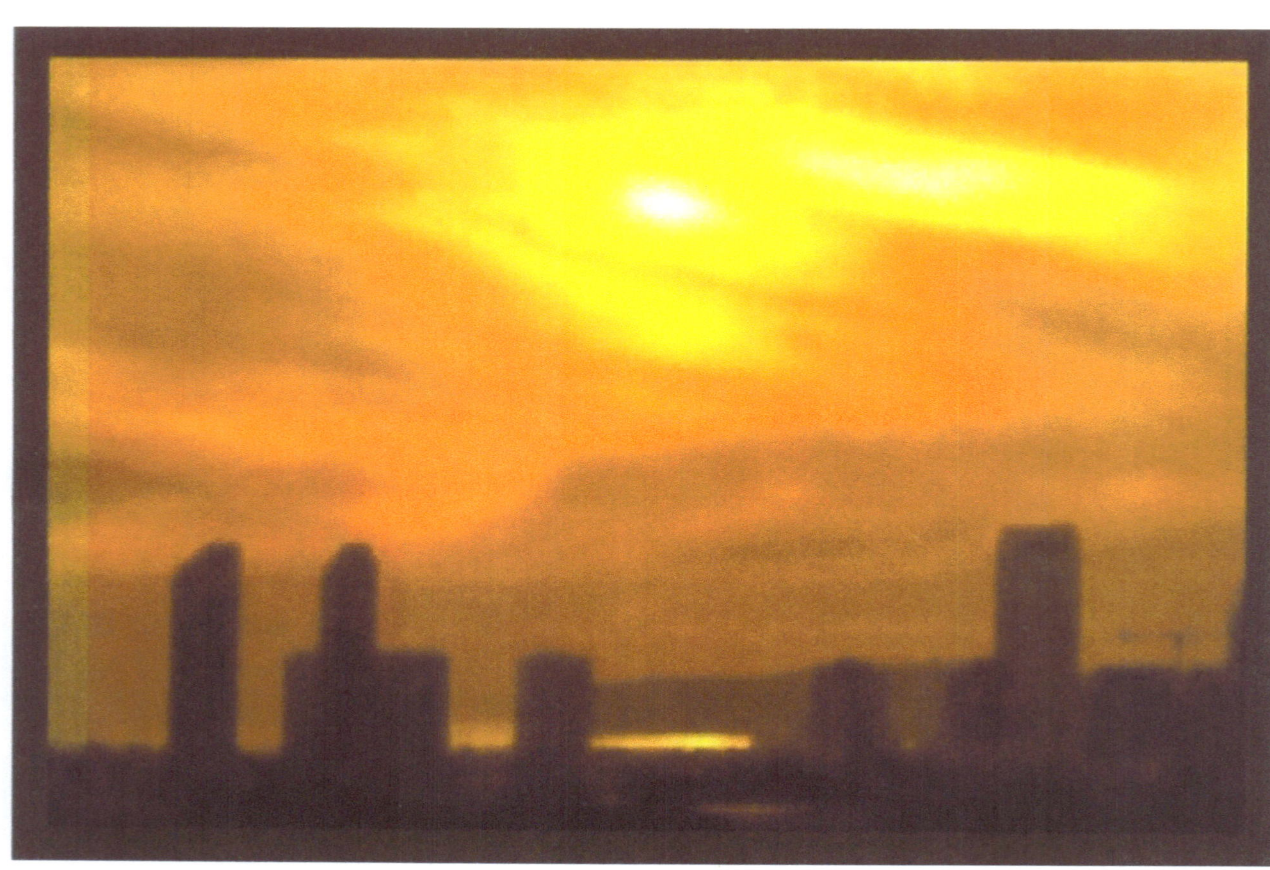

SUN DRUNK

Dumb sun, shine if you must, on my hair,
on the drunken rooftops, on the wine's nose,
on politics' dogged tongue. Everything is sick

with primary colors. Without conviction,
I lean on the Fifth Column, and pose in a gold
bikini for the Fourth Estate. Oh big white grape in the sky!

He kissed my left breast and left
for your blind day. Cry cognac into my mouth;
slake my thirsty love as you
have sated the moon's hunger. Do I fault

mammoth or tar pit? Ale
or addiction? Raise me up
with your orange fingers.
I will set on you.

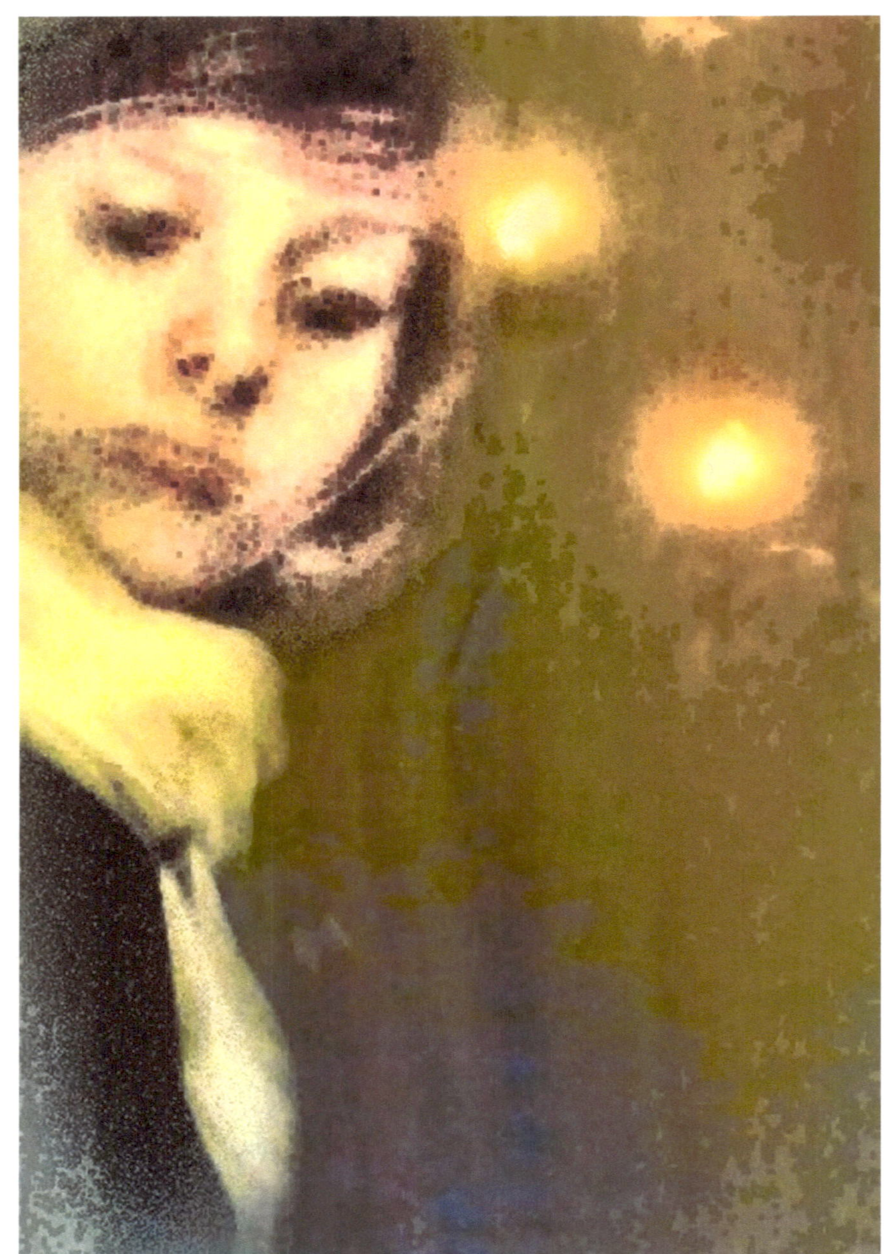

TANYA

Tanya, my paradise undone! Pouting
with both lips may have been your only virtue.
You wore that cream scarf like a haughty peasant,
my vagrant princess; oh!, see how my skin
sheds your rune and thickens in the dark. Now
that you're planting thorns in Nod, have you no
idea the hangovers, the hangnails chafing
my dreams awake to an aching neck? But you've
delicate nostrils and orange eyes and I might
forgive even your first disastrous lies,
if you resurrect my cold reflection with
this dawn. Tanya, my brief and pretty thief,
give back the heart you bribed with that gold skin;
oh, give me one last chance to surrender!

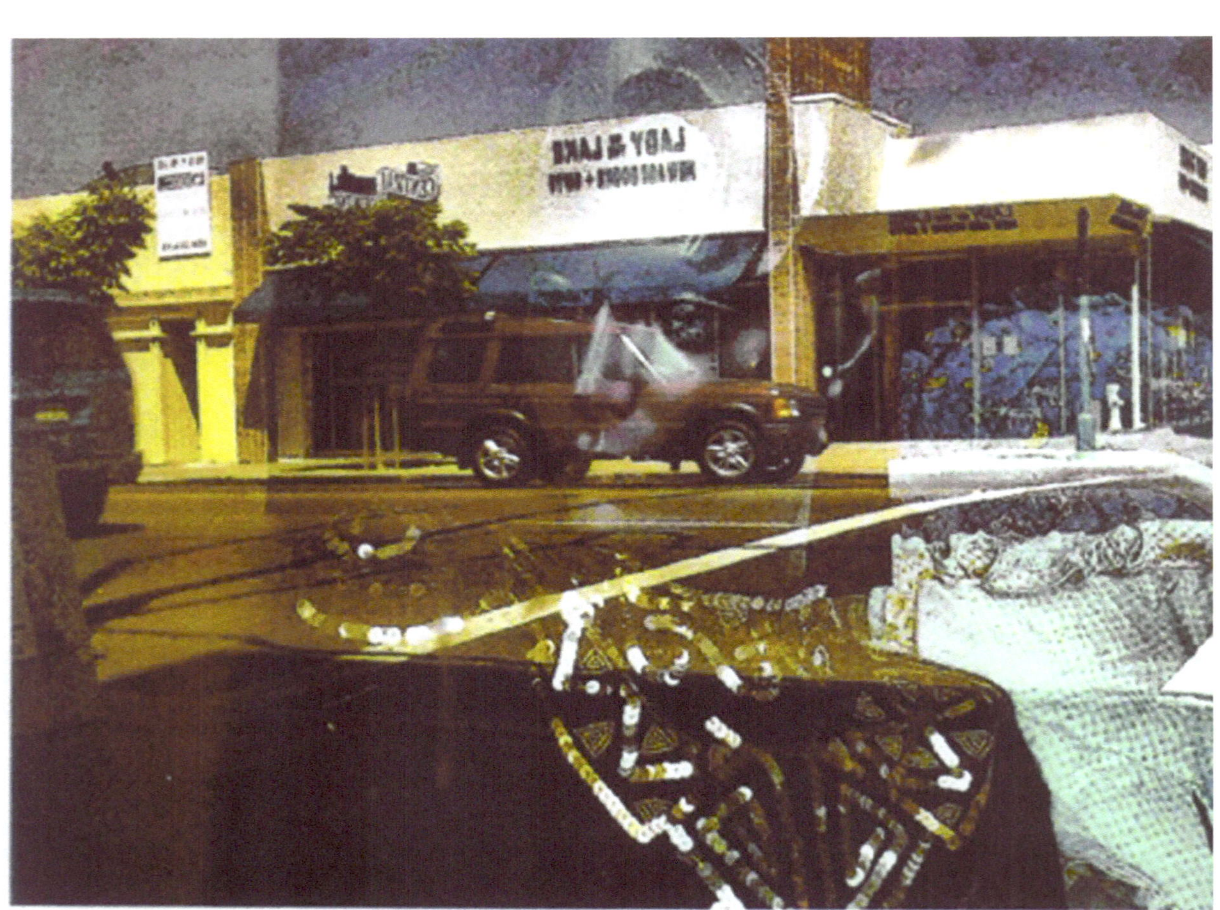

THE EYES OF THE MANNEQUIN

Through the eyes of the mannequin, through this shame-worn glass
I can see her duck as you drive to a stop. Her other heads
sprout still, sticking their spliced tongues out at the rain.

Love takes time; I mean it steals it. The sequins on my collar
boast radioactive dust. Children play at the edge of the curb,
eyeballs for marbles, stolen from women whose hearts stopped
like the arms of neglected cuckoos.

My ruffled pillow smells like the San Andreas fault, like random semen,
like bacon and aftershave. I've washed by hand all your excuses and polished
my nails blue. You falter, but I stand straight and numb. Oh, that I

were streetlight and not woman; that I could trade womb for motor,
blood for fuel. You taunt the serpents coiled around the bedpost, you mock
the perfect wave cascading down my forehead. And I could cast

a silent shadow on the motel's door. I could throw my limbs beneath
your wheels and leave the window washer with nothing to imagine.
To him I bequeath everything, and to every passerby.

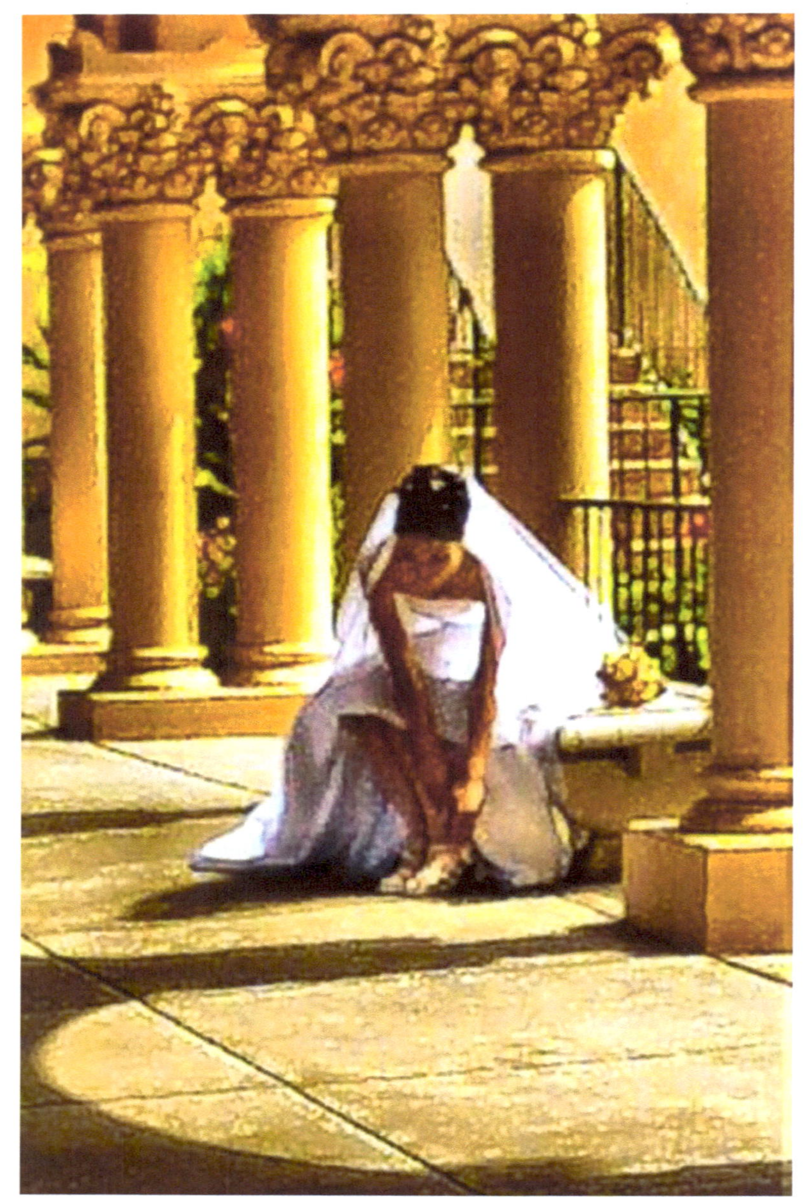

WAITING

All we do is to mask the waiting, as I wait for you
on summer's bench, slouched against the uselessness of words,
the walk-way riddled by the shadows of my shifting knees,

as you were waiting, while I laced my bridal gown slow as a waltz,
and the ticking of your watch echoed from the cathedral ceiling,
casting a maudlin pallor over Magdalene.

Bittersweet our most glorious honeymoon,
the testes, the children, and the heart. I woke

from your kiss, on the moon, to find the flag we planted against time
bleached in the sun.

Nothing can matter: not the unsaid prayers we've stacked in our closets,
not the oysters we've shucked. For death, still more slippery,
will not be confined to a shell.

Discard the unpink from our shrimp nets. Though we feast for a year,
the fading waves will herald death's repose.

You wrote:
Nature with a frugal eye
Asks only that we fuck, then die.
Our union only makes this more specific.

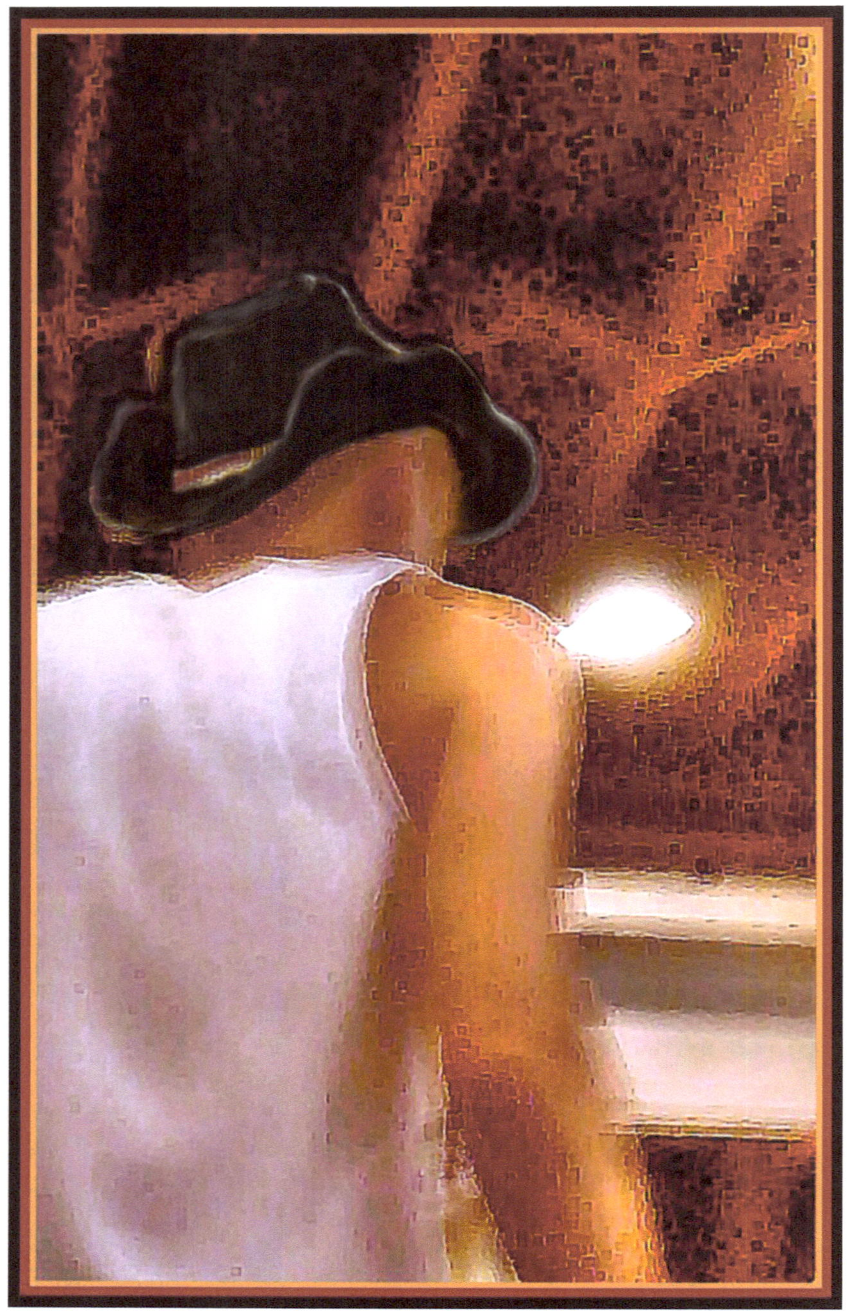

SONG FOR THE AIR *(SESTINA FOR JOHNNY)*

As I drift off, troubled by those more beautiful, I covet the air,
while still, dreamed shadows people this empty
and heavy room. In the half-hearted light
every woman's got a right to cry, to paint her room black
as Johnny Cash in one more cold hotel, and paint her eyes
blacker, now that he's laid to rest.

Only in Mama Bear's arms did he find rest.
Her kisses must have been seamless as the air,
for he was many things, but in his eyes
I could see that his heart was never empty.
Brave cowboys wear black;
they breathe the midnight song, but never hog the light,

and when they leave, their steps are light
and gentle on a woman's tears, unlike the rest,
slamming the doors and stomping toward the black
ends of a wannabe rambler. Too craven for the open air,
they crave only someone a little less empty
than themselves. Well, damn your eyes

if that man is you! And hello to he who eyes
me through the kitchen window, as I sing for light
on a faint day. What song cannot fill, will leave me empty
as a poor man's wallet, and my stone shall say: *Rest*

in peace, if you can. I ain't peddlin' nothin' here but air
and magic potion—pure, toxic, black

enough to make me curse again all your black-
outs, or make a drunk regret his whiskey, as I regret your eyes
last night. Oh, Johnny! How 'bout another one? The air
of sweet home in your voice will light
the long way back to Fort Worth, where I can rest
at last, while mom cooks posole to fill my empty

stomach. The heart is never empty
when there's something warm in the kitchen. I want black
pepper and a squirt of lemon in the broth; then rest
your head on me, if you need to, close your eyes
to the cruel wages of this art, and light
the way back up that candy mountain, with the air

Johnny has taken for his last, black breath. Rosemary fills the air.
Remember me, his eyes say, to all who listen and need rest.
Empty no more, we shall meet again in the light.

www.ingramcontent.com/pod-product-compliance
Lightning Source LLC
LaVergne TN
LVHW070148110826
845147LV00002B/345

* 9 7 8 0 9 7 7 4 0 0 0 1 0 *